WELCOME TO THE WORLD OF

Otters

Diane Swanson

WALRUS
B O O K S

Edited by Elizabeth McLean
Cover design by Steve Penner
Interior design by Margaret Ng
Typeset by Tanya Lloyd
Cover photograph by Thomas Kitchin/First Light
Photo credits: Glen and Rebecca Grambo/First Light iv; Robert Lankinen/First Light 2, 14, 20, 26; R.A. Clevenger/WL/First Light 4; Tim Christie 6, 18; Thomas Kitchin/First Light 8, 24; Jeff Foott 10; Weimann/First Light 12; Lynn Stone 16; Stanford/Agliolo/First Light 22

Printed and bound in Canada

Library and Archives Canada Cataloguing in Publication

Swanson, Diane, 1944–
    Welcome to the world of otters

    (Welcome to the world)
    Includes index.
    ISBN 1-55110-520-9
    ISBN 978-1-55110-520-8

    1. Otters—North America—Juvenile literature. I. Title. II. Series.
QL737.C25S92 1997   j599.74'447   C95-910733-1

For more information on this series and other Walrus Books and Whitecap Books titles, visit our web site at www.whitecap.ca

The publisher acknowledges the support of the Canada Council for the Arts and the Cultural Services Branch of the Government of British Columbia for our publishing program. We acknowledge the financial support of the Government of Canada through the Book Publishing Industry Development Program for our publishing activities.

Contents

World of Difference

OODLES OF ENERGY BUNDLED IN FUR. That's what otters are. Although they swim and hunt for food each day, they have plenty of pep left for play.

North America has two kinds of otters: river otters that weigh up to 14 kilograms (30 pounds) and sea otters that weigh two to three times more. Many sea otters are as big as large dogs.

River and sea otters have thick coats of mostly brownish-colored fur. That's what keeps them warm. Otters don't have much fat to protect them from the cold water.

To help them swim, otters have short

Eating well, these sea otters may live about 8 years. River otters may live more than 12.

1

Stiff whiskers sense movement, helping the river otter find prey underwater.

legs and webbed feet. The webbed toes on a sea otter's back feet are so long they form floppy flippers.

Underwater, special flaps of skin help both kinds of otters keep their ears dry. Special tails help them swim strongly. But the sea otter's wide, flat tail looks nothing like the river otter's thick, ropelike one.

Young river otters, called pups, live only with their mother until they are a few months old. Then their father joins the family. The otters travel and hunt together for about a year.

A sea otter pup lives only with its mother—not its father. But the mother and pup join other moms and pups, often floating in groups of up to 30. When sea otter pups are about eight months old—and almost fully grown—they usually head off on their own.

Plunk a penny on a sea otter and you cover about 250 000 hairs. There are less than half that many hairs on your whole head. Sea otter fur is so thick you can't push your fingers through it. In fact, it's the thickest fur in the world.

By holding masses of tiny air bubbles, the fur keeps sea otters warm in cold water. It also helps them float. But if the fur gets dirty, it cannot do its job. That's why sea otters clean themselves so often.

Where in the World

AN OTTER IN THE WATER IS ALWAYS RIGHT AT HOME. Sea otters spend their lives at sea, quite close to shore. Now and then, some clamber out onto rocks, but they are awkward on land. Many never leave the water at all. When sea otters sleep, they float on their backs—often among tall seaweed called kelp. Two or more otters may hold paws while they sleep.

River otters spend a lot of time in rivers and lakes, and in water along seashores. They are more graceful in the water, but they move well—and fast—on land. For short distances, they even outrun people.

Sleepy sea otters often wrap themselves in kelp to keep from drifting away.

5

**It's time out for
this river otter—
and a sunny rock
makes a great
place to rest.**

And river otters always sleep on land.
Wrapped around each other, they usually
rest in dens—under rocks, beneath tree
roots, or inside hollow logs.

In water and on land, river otters are
great travelers. They cover about 100
kilometres (60 miles) of waterways a year.
In winter, they often travel between these

waterways by sliding on ice and snow. Sometimes they tunnel through deep snow, keeping out of sight.

River otters once lived in most of North America. Today, they live mainly in Canada and Alaska, especially along the Pacific coast. Different kinds of river otters live on most other continents.

Sea otters once lived all around the north Pacific Ocean. Today, there aren't nearly as many as there were, and they live mostly along North America's Pacific coast.

OTTERS UP CLOSE

People working or living near water may spot river otters close by. Some otters snoop around docks, scramble over boats, and check out warehouses. Some even visit homes, poking around porches and peeking into windows.

One island family loved to watch river otters slide down a muddy hill near their house. The family even built the otters a special little house. But the otters preferred the family's house, nesting under the kitchen.

7

World Full of Food

The river otter hunts day or night, chewing its food—such as this trout—very well.

OTTERS NEED A LOT OF FOOD—fuel to keep them warm and busy. Each day, a sea otter eats food weighing one-fourth as much as the otter itself. It munches seaweed, but mostly it eats small sea animals, such as crabs, clams, and red sea urchins. An otter can turn its teeth and bones pink from eating so many of these urchins.

Diving for its dinner, the sea otter snatches food with its front paws. It may tuck some of its loot into pouchlike skin in its "armpits" and grab a rock. Back at the surface, the otter might use its teeth to crack crab shells. But it might need to use

9

After grabbing a tasty crab, this sea otter chows down.

the rock to break sea urchins open.

All through dinner, the sea otter cleans itself. It holds its food and rolls over to wash away any scraps. After dinner, it scrubs itself well.

The river otter eats berries and roots, but mostly it hunts animals. Using its nose and front feet, it digs in muddy river bottoms for crayfish, salamanders, and frogs. Or it dives—without a splash— and swims swiftly after fish. Sometimes it breaks dams built by beavers and grabs fish as the water level drops. Sometimes it even grabs young beavers. In winter, the otter hunts beneath ice that forms over water.

Several times a day, the river otter feasts. It gobbles up smaller snacks right in the water, but hauls bigger meals out. In its world full of food, the otter lives very well.

ESCAPE OF THE BEAVER

When a young beaver spotted two river otters swimming its way, it dove into the water. Then it hid beneath an old log on the bottom of the river.

The otters sniffed the riverbank where the beaver had been. They swam back and forth, hunting. When they headed away from the beaver, it rose among reeds to breathe. When they headed toward the beaver, it sank. Finally, the river otters moved on, and the beaver escaped.

11

World of Words

WHEN SOMETHING NEEDS SAYING, AN OTTER OUGHT TO SAY IT. And it usually does. The river otter snorts to warn other otters of danger. It hums to say, "I'm mad," humming louder and higher the madder it gets. If it becomes really angry—or very scared—the otter hisses. Sometimes it also SCREAMS.

But when a river otter feels comfortable, it grunts like a pig. It chuckles softly with other otters as they spend time together. And it chirps like a bird to make long-distance calls. On land or in water, "words" help otters stay in touch.

These river otters use grunts and chuckles to "talk" to each other.

13

The river otter uses its keen sense of smell to discover who has been by.

Like a river otter, a sea otter screams wildly if anything threatens it. Corner an otter and it snarls and barks like a dog. That's how a sea otter says, "Go away. Now."

When a mother sea otter dives for dinner, her pup usually has something to say about it. Left floating alone, it whines, then it makes a high-pitched, screaming cry. The sound is so loud it carries long distances. The pup has to be loud, or it can't be heard above the crashing of the ocean's waves. "Come back. I'm hungry and frightened," it is calling to its mother. She usually responds at once.

On her return, the mother coos softly to soothe her pup, cradling it high on her chest. Her coos turn to grunts when she starts to eat. But the contented sounds of her feeding soothe the pup, too.

NEWS WORTH SMELLING

River otters leave "smell-o-grams" for each other. With their front paws, they twist clumps of grass together. Then they sprinkle these twists with strong-smelling liquid from glands at their back ends. They also sprinkle bushes, stones, and clumps of dirt.

That's how an otter says, "This is my territory," or "I'm around here." A passing otter may sniff the news, then leave a "smell-o-gram" of its own—especially if it's looking for a mate.

New World

OTTER PUPS ARRIVE ALREADY WEARING THEIR FUR COATS. And at birth, sea otters even have their eyes open. They are perky little pups, usually born in watery beds of kelp—one otter to a mom.

Although its home is the water, a sea otter pup can't swim right away. It rides its mother, snuggling on her chest as she does the back float. There, the pup sleeps, stretches, and feeds. Rich, warm milk that flows from its mom helps the pup grow fast.

The mother otter cleans and dries her pup again and again. She coos all the while. But if eagles, killer whales, or people

Many sea otter pups, such as this one, arrive in winter. River otters often arrive in spring.

17

After leaving its den through an underwater "doorway," the river otter climbs onto a bank and shakes itself dry.

threaten her newborn, she grabs it with her front paws and dives underwater.

River otters are born on land—often in underground dens dug by other animals. The otter is not a good digger. Most dens have openings to let in fresh air, as well as the otters. But many dens also have under-water openings in the banks of streams or lakes. A tunnel leads from an underwater entrance up to a dry nesting "room" inside the den. There, on a blanket of leaves, grass, and moss, river otter pups are born. Often, two or three arrive at once.

Unlike sea otters, river otter newborns can't see for a few weeks. They stay tucked inside their den with their mom. For about three months, she suckles them, cleans them, and keeps them safe at home. She fights off any animal that tries to enter the den—including the pups' father.

FUSSY MAKES FLUFFY

It's a good thing a sea otter mom is so fussy. She must clean and dry her pup as soon as it is born—or it won't survive the cold at sea.

Lying on her back, the otter uses her front paws to roll her newborn over and over. She cleans it by licking and chewing its fur, and blows to help it dry. She works non-stop for nearly two hours until the fur is fluffy. Then the pup can keep warm, and the mother can rest for a bit.

Small World

LITTLE OTTERS HAVE LOTS TO
LEARN. They take lessons in swimming,
diving, fishing, and hunting. River otters
start learning as soon as they leave their
dens. The pups are usually afraid of water,
so their mother might let them hold onto
her when she swims. Or she might force
them to swim by tossing them into the
water—or diving with them on her back.

After a few days, the pups can swim well
on their backs, tummies, or sides. And when
their father joins them, the whole family
swims together. Often they travel one
behind the other, dipping and rising in

River otters
spend their
first winter
with their
families—and
discover snow.

21

Three sea otters cuddle in the kelp. One sniffs the air for danger. Sea otters also have good sight.

the water. Some people have mistaken a swimming otter family for a long, snakelike monster.

Both parents teach a river otter pup to find its dinner. They show it how to nose out food from muddy river bottoms. They train it to charge after a fish and trap it among the rocks. And all the time, they protect the pup from attacks by eagles, coyotes—even big fish.

A sea otter starts lessons as young as four weeks. When its mother hunts for food, she leaves her pup floating. At first, the pup just peeks underwater, watching her dive and swim. Then it tries—harder and harder—to follow her.

Soon, the pup can dive and swim. Then it goes exploring with its mom. It learns to find food and practices cracking open clams and sea urchins with rocks.

YOUNG AND WILD

One sea otter is lively. Two are trouble. Three or more? Look out! Young sea otters are so fired with energy they can't seem to stay still. They climb onto each other, their mothers, and sometimes human divers.

Sea otters push and pull other otters and nibble their tails. They feel, sniff, and lick every shell that they find. Even after hours of exploring, otters don't seem to tire. They just keep going, and going, and going…

23

Fun World

OTTERS HAVE FUN JUST BEING OTTERS. It's so easy for them to find food that they have plenty of time to play.

Like children, river otters often go sliding. They slide on snow and they slide on mud. They often slide down riverbanks on their tummies—splashing into the water at the bottom.

Another otter game is hide-and-seek. One river otter dives into the snow and tunnels underneath. A second river otter noses into the snow here and there, looking for the first otter. Sometimes the hidden otter pokes its head out, squeals, then hides

"What will I do next?" this sea otter seems to say. It plays so many games in the water.

25

This river otter is looking for its playmate. The otter spots moving animals easily.

again. If it's caught, the two otters usually play fight.

River otters also play with toys. They juggle sticks or pebbles with their front paws—or balance these toys on their noses. Sometimes a river otter hides a fish—like a toy—in the grass. Another otter uses its super sense of smell to sniff out the fish, then hides it for the next otter.

Sea otters play with toys, too. They push or climb on bits of floating wood. They use their front paws to toss and catch seaweed and shells.

One pup may play with another pup or its mother. The two tumble and roll together. They nibble each other's ears and feet. Sometimes they jump right out of the water together.

Games like these help keep both sea and river otters strong, healthy, and ready to hunt. But the games are also just plain fun.

AWESOME OTTERS

Otters often surprise people. Here are some of the reasons why:

- A sea otter can dive 90 metres (300 feet) under the sea.
- A river otter can stand on its two back legs—using its tail as a prop.
- To avoid freezing, wet river otters dry themselves by rolling in powdery snow.
- To flush dirt from their fur, sea otters flip somersaults in the water.

Index